FROM PAIN TO POETRY

A Collection of Spoken Word

BY GWEN DANWOOD

Volume 1

Attention: Permissions Coordinator

Welcome To The Storm Publishing!
info@w2tspublishing.net

Ordering Information:
Quantity sales. Special discounts are available on quantity purchases by corporations, associations, and others. For details, contact the publisher at the email address above.

Orders by U.S. trade bookstores and wholesalers.

ISBN: 978-1-966612-59-9

Cover Design: Olaniyan Bukola

Veronica Miller, Red Diamond Editing by V. Rena,

First Printed Edition: September 2025

Printed in the United States of America

Table of Contents

Acknowledgements

I am extremely thankful to God for giving me the grace to write, and the courage to share. I want to thank my mother and father who sacrificed and taught me all the "life nuggets" of wisdom they had, and for doing the very best they could in my life. I love you dearly.

I want to thank my elementary English teacher who introduced me to a poem by my favorite poet Edgar Allan Poe. The encounter with his work still remains with me today. I also want to thank my God-given team of destiny helpers, and all those who support me. Thank you.

Knock Out

I don't want to be seen!
No! No more.
Can't I do it behind the scenes?
No! No more.

Fear of the people,
Fear of the pressure.
Get your mind right,
Put on the Blesser.

Speak what He says—speak!
Do what He says—do!
It's in His power,
He has equipped you.

Fear of rejection,
Please, it's like a disease,
Trampled by Jesus' blood.

Now, go,
You can do all things through Christ, you see.

Limitations—knocked out!
Low self-esteem—knocked out!
Unfruitful mindsets—knocked out!

Champion, arise!
Roaring inside,
Hold your head high!
Hold your head high!

Breathe in and out.
Let go of doubt
As He sends you out.

Salvation is calling;
Salvation is coming,
So stop wasting time as if...
The unexpected hour won't come.

No more hiding!
Launch out!

Chains

Oh, these chains,
they are fallin' of me...
Oh, these chains,
they are fallin' off of me,

Oh, these chains.

Boisterous waves cannot cease
Unless you speak.

Speak.

Silence the voices of
Doubt, worry, anxiety, and unbelief—
All workers of fear,
Plaguing my brain,
Speakin' louder
To make me hostage to defeat.

But-
Silence the voices.
Speak, peace, be still!

Oh yes, this is real!
It's happening!

Oh! I can hear the sounds of the chains—
They are falling off of me!
I can hear the sound of the chains—
They are falling off of me!

Those chains that were wrecking my brain.
But, Sal...vation has come.
No, I'm not ashamed.
No, I'm not ashamed.
No more chains.

Dance Moves

I decided to dance.
I moved my arms like waves
On a beach.
Created feelings inside of me,
That moved my feet.
I decided to dance.

Though these days in this here life
Aren't always smooth,
I decided to dance—
Dance and groove.

I decided to dance.

Pain in my hands.
Pain in my feet.
I still decided to dance.

Dance, Dance
Dance and groove.

See ah,
Time for this and a time for that,
Even a time to combat
These sorrows of life
That just ain't nice—
But that's alright.

I decided to dance.
Dance for my change.

I decided to dance.
With flags in my hands,
I praised and danced.
I decided to dance.

Dance for my joy,
Dance for my peace,
Dance and dance,
Moving rhythmically to life's beat.

I feel the presence of Jesus
All over me
When I decided to move and dance.
I decided to dance.

Flight

Just... when I felt like it was over.
Just... when I felt I couldn't go anymore.
That's when the power of God kick...ed in,
Fuelin' my heart like never before with strength!

Causing my
Eagles wings to soar
More and more.

Higher and
Higher and
Higher,
Tell I reached my flight.

Ooo, and things are gettin' brighter
And brighter.

Spirit of defeat,
Watch me soar.

Inspired To Do

I arose this morning,
And the words began to flow—
Not on my own, but by the living streams of the Holy Ghost.

So, I went to writing
As He began to speak,
Words readily coming from the throne room.

He wanted me to put them in ink.
I... didn't have to think about anything.

All I had to do was write,

Announcing every word that I heard just right,
Prophetically driven in God's mission,
As the magnifying glass vision appeared before my eyes.

I had to make a decision—
Stop and obey Him as His words made an incision into my heart,
For those who are
sufferin' and bleedin'
And feel like their life is fallin' apart.
That is what I am inspired to do.

Sight

I see the sun arising,
Even though
I'm suffering.

I see the sun arising,
Even though these
Nimbostratus,
Cumulonimbus
Clouds are hovering over me.

I still see the sun arising,
All around me.

I see the sun arising,
Even though raindrops are fallin' on my face.

I see the sun arising.
Faith, joy, peace spring inside me.
Today! Speaking to me.

I see the sun arising,
Even though Satan keeps
Plottin', ployin', and playin' these games,
Trying to destroy me.

I still see the sun arising...
My Savior intercedes for me.
I see the sun arising.
Arising!
Arising!

The purpose of my life is quite fitting.
I see the Son arising.
S-O-N,
SON! Arising!

Got my feet to dancing, dancing, dancing
Cause I see the sun,
Arising.

This Father of Mine

Sounds of the song
Just keep on
Playin' in my head.

 Oh, Abba Father,
He's like no other,
Like no other.
Oh, Abba Father.

Oh, Abba Father,
He's like no other,
Like no other.
Oh, Abba Father.

This Father of mine...
He's something else, you see,
Rearranging my mind,
Causing my cloudy eyes to see.

This Father of mine...
He's definitely a keeper,
Far greater than a stripper.

This Father of mine...
Oh, I love Him.
Oh, yes indeed!

Because He first loved me,
 He gave me
His only begotten Son that came and saved me.

He saved me from the lustful desires that I had for
another.
But... no more late-night dates with
Imaginations of fake fantasies
That draw my mind from the truth of reality.

Leading me to the grave,
And keeping me a slave,
And wasting my time!

 Surely, I must tell you,

This Father of mine...
He's something else, you see.
If He delivered me,
Surely, He can set you free.

Yes! This Father of mine...
He's something else, you see.

Words

The words that you speak
Are an anointing oil that heals me.
A peaceful river flows.
When you speak your words,
Your words,
Your words,
Is like a time bomb
That destroys
The walls
I built up for so many years,
As my entire circulatory system receives your blood therapy,
Killing dangerous cells that could have caused...
My very heart to stop beating.

Your words.

Speak, Jesus.
Speak... to me.

Your words light up my feet
To the path you have for me—
Free!
Your words that you give me are right.
They're alrighter...
Reminding me how much you love me,
As they fighta! Fighta! All kinds of wrong mindsets,
intellects, and Amalekites.

Your words,
 Your words,
 Have power!
Even in the darkest hours.

They shatter! Shatter!
They make my heart patta patta for more of Thee...

Your words are like thunder,
Cracklin' through my inner forest.
As your words sound out—
You're the Lion of Judah—Roar!

Your words, they get one's attention,
And oh, not to mention words...

Your words are fitting and so sweet
When I eat!
When I eat!
They nourish my very soul to sleep.

Your words...
Your words... Jesus.
 Your words!
They cause me to fall to my knees.

Your words.
Your words are life to me.

Well Woman

A well woman
Is not a Hell woman.

She knows how to speak to her man,
Hold his hand,
Be his friend—
A loving companion,
As she supports and cheers for him.

She is a righteous leader,
As she wears her letterman jacket with the Be
Attitudes.

This woman knows what to do.

A well woman
Is not a Hell woman.
She... is happy and holy,
As she joyfully serves him.

She makes him proud to announce to everyone in the
crowd
That she is his wo...man—
Cause she *wow's* him not with her charm,
But with her inner beauty of humility,
A pure heart and sincerity,
Filled with generosity,
Working diligently with her hands,
Prayin', prayin', and prayin' for him—her man.

A well woman is not a Hell woman.
She knows what to do—
Build him up,
And let her life song host the melody of true love
That translates: "I got you."

You see,
A well woman is not a Hell woman.

Her man—
Her man can rest on her chest when he's faced with
life's test.

A well woman is not a Hell woman.
She provides security for her man to share
transparently
Only things he wants to speak to her—and not others—
For she is not a gossip queen.

A well woman
Is not a Hell woman.

She is a Proverbs 31 woman, you see.

A well woman
Is not a Hell woman.

She is all God called her to be.

So, you love her

So, you saw a pretty face,
But never took the time to meditate
 On the very image that got you hooked,
Like a cover of a book.
Failing to go deep inside to look...
To see what's goin' on in the chapters of this woman,
Where her true beauty is captured?

 But instead, you only took a look—like a cover of a
book.
Never getting to the true essence inside.

All you wanted to do was just
Take her emotions on a rollercoaster ride,
To see how far you can get without turning the pages.

Fakin' like you read her,
But you were only skimming through the pages.

So, you say you love her?

You don't even know her.
Your sight for her is just...
A piece of meat,
As you pretend like Judas, kissing her on the cheek.

So, you say you love her?

Brother, there's no truth in you!
You go from one mind game to another—
To where you make yourself think your lies are true.

So, you love her?

False declarations, saying you care.
Then, why you're on the internet and around town,
Having romantic cuddling sessions
And being other women's teddy bear?

Oh! And in their garments too!
But you say that you uh… love her?

Oh! You Mr. Do Right!
There is no truth in you.
Cause you only took a look—like a cover on a book.
Your lies and deceit have been exposed!

So, you say that you love…
Your words, actions, and deeds have spoken,
Treatin' her like an unwanted token.
Thou after being with you,
The fruit of your love is bearin' its tree,
As she is broken.

But no worries, you see,
Cause you failed to read the climax of her story.
No more victim of your cruelty.
She is healed, saved, and restored by the King.

So, you love her?
You just lost a virtuous woman.

So, you love her? Wait!
Now… that she is restored, you want to come back, my friend?

Rewind!

Then, let me grab the mic and let me say this again—

So, you love her?

There's no more playin' double dutch with her heart,
A virtuous woman always wins in the end.

Friend

A friend one should treasure.
Finding value in her,
Rubies, pearls, and diamonds cannot compare.

A friend to share life's intimate matters,
And the care of her,
She won't tell anyone else the matters.
She fuels friendship with the red rose of confidentiality.

Her love shows bright because the Son of God lives within her.
That's the reason she can stick by me through thick and thin.

A friend to be treasured.
Though distance may grow between you and me,
Your voice will always echo these kind words you spoke to me:

I love you.

You're a friend I do treasure.
Friend.

A Mother's Hands

A mother's hands are utilized all day,
Extended to those in need—
To be loved in a very special way.

A mother's hands;
How gentle they can be...
Being extended to those that may have offended them.

A mother's hands
Are to be treasured, yes indeed.

A mother's hands—
A gift from God that all will know and learn to understand,
Even as she ages.

A mother's hands,
Full of worth, year after year.
A mother's hands.

How precious are your hands, Mother,
How precious are your hands.

As you are here, and even as you transition on,
The work of your hands will continue on.

Be It Not To Be

I judge no one.
Do I see the heart behind the man?
Do I see the heart of the one that has been trampled on again
and again?
I judge no one.

Whether jealousy or envy—
It might be there,
But...
I judge no one,
Cause it could be me there.

I judge no one.
Only the Omnipotent One can truly see and understand
A heart that has been abused.
So, I choose not to use the enemy's tool,
I judge no one.

But instead,
I pray for everyone.

Eyes, A Wanderer

Eyes wander off...
Drifting to places afar,
Not noticing the driving of thy soul,

As my eyes wander to places untold.
Eyes wanderer...
Look there and see,
These eyes that wander, causing death to seek after me.

Eyes wanderer...
That cause my life of royalty to turn to dust, being controlled by thee.
Eyes wanderer... not yielding to the Holy Ghost.
Eyes wanderer.

Feelings of shame cause eyes a wanderer.
Is there hope for me?
Trapped as I wander,
Wanting desperately to be set free,
As my eyes wander.

He Knows

He knows my name.
So, why do I fear?
As the terrors of this world lay and wait,
So near—whispering in my ear,
Words of despair here and there.
Why should I care?
He knows my name.
Though darkness is all around me,
He knows my name.
Fear keeps trying to drown me!
He knows my name.
So, why should I be afraid?
When I box with inner voices
In the break of war,
That try to sell me defeat,
He knows my name.
No! I don't take on the image and nature
Or the mark of the beast.
I hold firm to the very essence of my Creator.
He knows my name.
His victory reigns.
He knows my name.
Cause His love—it frees me.
While I stand in this test,
I must confess,
I must confess...
Truly, only faith behooves me.
He knows my name.

My Soul

Oh, how can this soul of mine win, being so out of control?
Wanting rest but never standing the test,
Lusting for life's pleasures that always... seem like gold.

As the frequency of sound increases—
Waving more, more, and more...

Can I find rest for my yearning soul?
Can anybody hear clearer my cry?

Spirit of God on a bass guitar screaming,
He will win.
When I want to bend,
I lean in... lean in,
Yielding to the Greater One within.

As this oh soul won't live out of control...
It lives holy.

Sometimes

Sometimes, in life,
We think we know all—
Just to find out we know not.

I thought I was being the best wife to you,
But I discovered at times I have not.
You are so precious to me,
Even when I was blinded with my perspectives
And I couldn't see
You were sent to help me, even when I didn't know me.

So, at times I have ignored
Your drawings on my heart board of truth—
Even when it hurt.
The truth, you see, is my reality
That I failed to see.

Please, forgive me.
Though I have caught the revelation late,
I'm still a saint,
doesn't mean I have it all together,
But this one thing I know:

In life, sometimes,
We can all be misunderstood.
Thank you—sometimes, and every time,
You tell the truth to me.

Simply Plain

I woke up with my right mind;
I got every limb functioning properly,
Knowing that my God is always on top of me,
The lover of my soul that provides for me everything I need.

In my daily struggles,
No, I won't complain.
It's simple and plain.

Always there for me,
Working things out for my good.
His love's so real;
It's simple and plain.

Strengthening me with His grace,
To help me face every adversary that tries to attack me.
It's simple and plain.

My mind, body, soul, and spirit,
No, you won't be drained,
For when Jesus has made it plain,
He's the God that's for me.
With all power, He reigns.

It's simple and plain.

Hand

I can see you holding my hand,
Not through the naked eye's lens.
I see your hand directing me to the places of Jubilee.
I see your hand—no, not as a magician,
But as a loving friend,
Performing breakthroughs and miracles;
While still holding my hand,
Protecting me,
And keeping me from falling into life's trials of quicksand.

I see your hand.
Your mighty hand.

The Fight for Freedom

No other gift that I know
Than the gift of freedom.

Freedom to live.
Freedom to dance.
Freedom of choice.
Freedom of voice.

Freedom.

No other gift can stand
For justice for all,
To all that will take heed.

Freedom in the Merismos Man
That gave His life for thee.

Freedom for which He stands—
For all nations and for all that will
Raise their hand and yield their heart.
Yes, to that Man—
Freedom, liberty for which He stands.

Lit torch that beams so bright,
Calling those out of darkness
To His marvelous light.

Freedom!
What great gift that comes from Thee,
Freedom for all to receive!

Yes, Jesus is the Merismos Man.
In Him, there is true liberty and freedom,
For which He stands,
Extending His hands.

Yes, it's Jesus!
The Merismos Man.

Who Am I

I looked in the mirror, and what did I see?
I didn't see reality looking at me.
I saw glamour, and I saw fame.
I saw an image that had forgotten its name.

I looked in the mirror, and I didn't see myself.
I didn't see the *me* that was looking at me.
I saw him, I saw them, and I even saw *they*—
But I didn't see the beast
That was eating the beauty of my insides away.

Like the Scribes and Pharisees,
I failed to take heed to the voice of Jesus saying,
"He that is without sin among you,
Let him cast the first stone."

You are not God,
So leave my people alone.

So, who is that in the mirror
That has now been revealed?
It is me,
the hidden message revealed

Cast not a stone.

Will You Be Ready

Will you be ready?
The days are growing shorter,
And hearts are going colder—
Not knowing that salvation is near.

Though love is a knockin',
Still, some will not let Him in.
Now, this is what is written,
So the mystery is not hidden
To those that would not let Him be their friend.

Instead, they refuse to repent,
Stay captive to their sins.

Who knows the time or can predict the hour?
But like a thief in the night,
He will come.

No, don't waste another moment.
Don't waste another hour,
Stop the debate

Will you be ready when Jesus comes?

He Speak, I Speak, Spoken

These words are not idol.
Go, check the report—
Purposefully inspired
To be hired,
To write and speak to all men.

Words that aren't idol—
They can start a revival.

His words He speaks, I speak too.
Devotionally paired,
He speak. I speak.

Spoken.
Words of truth.

Beauty Comin'

As I wallow in my sorrows,
My unending cries keep drippin' down my face.
And though they are a-drippin',
The grateful beauty will soon spring—
Bursting with abundance.

Beauty is coming.

So, I'll rise up with my soul a-leapin',
With proper speech… relax and be still.
The plans God has to prosper you is real.
He knows how you feel.

So, chill, and sip on the lemonade.
These hot and fiery situations will soon pass away.

Like a winner of a pageant, you'll get your sash,
And His glory will be seen as you pass
Through the test.

Go ahead and practice your wave—
Cause there's beauty for ashes.
Beauty is comin'..

Night Whispers

Strange whispers hollin' in the night,
Giving feet to my fears.
But oh, fear, hear—
Faith drawth near,
As my ear leans to hear
My Savior clear,
Telling me:

Rest, my dear.
Lay your head on your pillow.
Don't worry about tomorrow.
Take no thought of fear.
I am here.
I am here for you.

Just speak my word,
And the stranger's voices will disappear.

Hold on, my dear.
Hold on, my dear,
And let go of your worry pillow.
Go ahead and cheer—
I am right here.

Let my word billow.
Hear the strange voices disappear.
Heaven on earth appears,
For you, my dear,
It is made clear,
My word is the answer,

Even in the night.

Get on Walking

I see the lit path for me.
And I'm gonna take it—no more sitting here in this
Idolville.
Ain't no more for me.

My soul is always thirstin' for greater.
That old undertaker, excited and delighted
To bury the dead sinner of me.

I gotta get on walking;
The wider road isn't better,
For it leads to hell, condemnation, and damnation.

Oh Jesus, hear my voice!
I want to get it to-get-there,
Cause I hear out there the righteous ones speakin':
Soon that day will come,
And I want my soul to be won... by you.

I give you my heart, Jesus;
I see...
Breaking forth to the lit path of new life.

From Idolville to holiness,
My soul finds its quenched thirsty rest in you.

The Great Damascus experience—
Sinner to saint,
Heavenly-bound living,
Receiving all blessings God's giving.

As I travel here,
The road lit that God prepared for me
In my new residency.

Breaking forth to the lit path of new life—
To holiness,
As my soul finds its thirst fill in you.

Great Damascus.
Saint-a locus.
Heavenly-bound living in truth.
Blessings found as I travel
In my residency of peace.

Loving to Be Loved

My life was void.
Darkness prevailed, and I wasn't well.
Till your love came in and covered my sin,
And made me win.

You broke hell's chains off of me,
And set my heart, mind, and soul free!

It was your love, Jesus.
Your love, Jesus, is greater than the world could ever be to me…
Giving me true security.

Your love changed me!
What an awesome ability to me…

Hallelujah to you, Most High!
Thank you for demonstrating your love to… me.

Oh, I'm so thankful and forever grateful
That you thought about… me,
As you bled and died so that I would not be despised.

Thank you for your love, Jesus.
You give to me unconditionally,
And that places my soul at peace.

For your love, Jesus…
Thank you for your love.

Weight!

Weight! Weight! Weight!
Heavy burdens weighing me down continuously;
Got no more business doing business—
In this here mournin',
Noon hours,
Evening hours,
Nor in the midnight hours.

Producing a yoke on my soul God hasn't given me...

It's time to take a minute and no longer,
Wait another minute.

It's time to be free,
Free from the weight of these heavy burdens
That are plaguing me.

Blues Bench

I sat on that bench of blues.
Sadness enveloped me.
Many men having their chance at
Multiple times of my soul death execution
At the bench of blues.

Crying nights in sorrow,
Hoping for a better tomorrow—
Only to find myself
back on the blue bench of blues.

Bench blues.
Bench blues.
How can one escape you?
Sometimes coming out one by one,
And two by two.

Bench blues.
People don't understand you.
"Just get off the flight," they say—
Like it's just that easy.
Not understanding this war zone
Faced day after day after day after day.

Blue bench blues.
Lonely as can be.
Blue bench blues
Trapped.

Yet, joy will overthrow you,

your blue bench blues.

No longer will I be abused.

Wrestling to Escape

How to escape these wrong fantasies inside of me,
Caught in flames that cost.
Cruising down memory lane—
Insanity!

Wrong visions and emotions feasting and festering in my soul.
These enemies of memories—
How can I control?

Hard to explain
Why I entertain the insanity game,
While my past keeps haunting my name.

I have to escape from thee.
Trapped in these fantasies inside of me,
As I am caught in the flames
Of memory's game.

Insanity!
Feasting at me,
As my soul drifts away to the enemy's lanes.

Lost all control—
Hard to explain
Why I entertain this destructive fame
That keeps callin' my name,
Callin' my name.

I want to be free.
Want to be free.
Jesus, come and save me.

Scène

Tree leaves dancing with the breeze, as the
sounds of nature—voices with sweet melodies
That put my soul at ease.

Midsummer skies,
Beauty before my eyes.
Rowin' with vines on the fences
As I walk by.

Radiantly cool to me—
Green trees with leaves
Dancing with the breeze…

A beautiful scene.

Mother

Well, let me just say,
She is far beyond her mistakes.

Listen—my mother.
She is a mother, mothering, mother.
In my eyes, she is like no other—
Preserver, Paratrooper.
Jumps through hoops, children.
A multitasking one.

Well, let me just say—
Oh! She is a mother, mothering, mother.

Make no mistake about it!
Mess with one of her babies, and she will be 'bout it,
'bout it.
Slayin' dragons.
Yes!! She gets it done!

Well, let me just say,
I'm gonna tell you right today.

She makes her rounds baking us homemade bread.
Oh yes, my mother—
She be in the kitchen doing her thang—
Fryin' her chicken and cookin' her collard gran's,
And cornbread—that's how we were fed.

Well, let me just say—
To the highs and the lows,
Extra, extra, extra away.

My mother—she is a mother, mothering, mother.
Beauty queen, always on top of her game.
Makeup ready, holding it steady,
With her clothes looking sharp,
Nice and pret...ta, pret...ta

At every stage of life.
That's right... teens, 20s, 30s, 40s—
Oh yes! Even 50s, 60s, and 70s too.

Daddy, you know what to do?
Appreciate her because God gave her to you.

A virtuous woman with the Word,
Who taught the Word, and lived the Word,
And consistently instilled in - her children—God's truth.

As the echo of her legacy
To keep Jesus first still rings in our ears...

My mother—
I said my mother!
She is a mother, mothering, mother,
Who did what she had to do.

That's *my* mother.
And I do love her,
And I will forever be her daughter too.

I celebrate my mother.

Speak One

I speak...
Release the words inside of me, my God has given.
No more fear.

I speak...
Rhythmic words flowing from my lips—
Sounds so sweet,
And meanings so deep.

I speak...
Visions and melodies,
I speak.

Yes, I speak...
Right fitting words that speak to the soul.
Make ears hear, eyes see, and hearts receive poetic sounds.

As I release—
I speak.

Change In the Chains

There is the change in the chains
That release the bond of trauma trapped inside of me.

Why does death speak its defeat?
The Greater has appeared.

Goodbye, dear—
This is my year!

As my feet go leaping in Jubilee's Jambalaya song,
Keep leapin' in free—
Sweet change in the chains to me,
in Jesus, my Joy Spring.

Urgency to Him

I gotta to have Him.
I gotta to see Him.
Heard His name is Jesus Christ—
The True and Living God.

Oh! I got to have Him!
I got to see Him...
Living life way beyond the clouds.

Oh, I got to have Him.
I gotta to have Him in this hour,
Before my time here
Will no longer be a mystery.

This is an urgency—
I got to have Him.

Lying

I was lying with a man
Who wasn't lying with me.
Bodily present,
Not Heavenly sent.

I was lying with a man
That wasn't lying with me.

He fulfilled his assignment
As he spoke words in my ears—
Words that I...
I loved to hear.
Sounded like melodies in my ear,
Sounded like a great symphony
With sweet harmonies.

But he only left me
Empty, lonely,
And a broken me.

Why couldn't I see?
I was lying with a man
That wasn't lying with me.

He got his fill
And told me his will
As he looked me... right in my face,
Speaking those gut-wrenching words
That flowed from his lips
Like it was a piece of cake for him to fake—
Telling me, "I wasn't the one for him,"
While still taking the best of me.

I was lying with a man
Who wasn't lying with me.

Tired of doing this
Over and over again—

Lying with a man
That wasn't meant for me.

Offended

As I search my soul,
Discovering wrong,
I learned I have been here too long.

Church hurt is real.
Is there anyone else who knows how I feel?
Saved, sanctified,
Tired of them doing what they do.

Where is the gospel sermon—
"I love you"?

So full of shame,
I get the blame.

Wait...
Aren't they accountable too?

Can't walk away—
Too much at stake.

Let's talk it through,
Destroy this fence,
And do what we were meant to do—

Forgive.

Speak All

Speak to me.
Release the words God said to thee.
Release and speak...
Right fitting words that we heard,
Rhythmically flowin' from our lips, you see.
Sound so sweet,
Meanings so deep—
Speak.

Speak with our hands artistically.
Visions and melodies to the hearts and the minds,
As poetic sounds make their rounds, right on time.

Release.
Speak.

Flee Da Dee Dum

Every time I get to the great road that beams light,
It appears that something quickly draws me
To the places that I don't want to be.

There is a war going on inside of me—
Wanting to be free;
While the word He spoke to me keeps echoing in my
head.

Even though within my very soul,
I know that an ungodly unity put shackles on my life.

How can someone that knows what to do that is right—
Yet run... to that dreary place time and time again?

My soul is in grief, like a newly widowed woman,
Wondering why I had to lose
And be clothed in this here blues.

I wish I could have told that brother to take his walking
shoes,
didn't ask for a congregational party
for those that have not kissed the covenant vows of
holy matrimony.

It has happened again—
Pretending to be friends,
When we both knew what we were doing was
committing sin,
Again and again.

How could... I think I could win?

His stories were a toy for me,
And even for her—I didn't see.

Adultery.

Oh, my pitiful soul,
Why did I lose it out of control...?

Living back in slavery's sin;
Gender arrested.

When the violence festered up,
Why did they put me... in cuffs
When it wasn't only me?

Generational bad movies hit on repeat.
Yes, it's time to flee the Da Dee Dum
Before Judgment Day comes.

Lord Jesus, save me.

Forgiveness in The Family

Forgiveness in family—
That is best to do.

Forgiveness in family
Releases the kinder part of you.

Forgiveness in family,
Oh! What a treat!

Forgiveness in family—
Let the fighting cease.

Forgiveness in family;
That's what true love will do.
Forgiveness brings peace and harmony too.

Whether near or far,
Forgiveness lets others know who you are—
A giver indeed of God's great gifts:
Love and mercy.

Forgiveness in family—
That's how to live.

Forgiveness in family—
It's good for you and good for me.

Forgiveness.

Lily Dance

I tried dancing with the lily,
But the lily didn't want to dance with me.

The Art of Aging

There's the beauty in the art of your age.
Clay has its change,
As it's upon the wheel.
Cracks sometimes tailor-made
For the beautiful piece of art to be displayed.

Woman, do you know
There is art in your age?
Nothing is meant to stay the same.

Go ahead and strut on life's stage.
There's the beauty in the art of your age.

You Overcomer

Girl!!
I have been waiting for you to arrive here.

You sat back.
You stayed silent.
You didn't believe in yourself.
You kept feeling that you weren't enough,
Measuring yourself up with your own and others' measuring
tape.

Yeah, you procrastinated.
You let fear hold you back.
You got spat on
And stabbed in the back numerous times,
Shamed and rejected.
Being misunderstood was in your hood.

But girl... that Champion inside of you
Wouldn't let you give in.
He cheered you along to the very end.

Now, look at you!
Walking with those feet lit
With the gospel,
As your mouth speaks,
Letting others know what's poss...ible
Through Him that strengthens thee.

Man, wooo... we... look at you doing new things!
Wait...! Wait...! Is that a new ring?!

Girl, Jesus done, done His thing!

For sure—
You're an Overcomer.

Purpose

Tired of unhidden dreams being seen.
Simply confused.
I didn't know what to do.

So, I prayed to the Master
About my inner disaster—
Of the fog overtaking my clarity,
And why my purpose on Earth
Is such a mystery to me.

As it appeared, I was opportunity niche hoppin'
While still holding on to the gift of creativity,
Waiting to share.
But do I dare?

Repeating cycles of even lost dreams.
Yet, I kept on driving as thoughts came over my mind—
Get off this time.

Feet led by Heaven's guide,
Surely divine.

A place prepared for me that I didn't expect to see,
An applauded seat
Waiting for me to arrive—
To my surprise.

The Driven Path

Seen by the,
Creator's creation, in Him I glean,
To the path lit still as He ordered my feet.
With the rhyme of poetic filled clarity
A joyful discovered as I
Walk the driven path lit for me.

Arts Community

Artsy community,
Prospering in unity.
One heart, one mind
With the sound of poetry—
As others hear your voice.

Holding

Anchor planted,
Stop the sail.
Overwhelmed, but I won't let go of you.

You walk me through the crowded road,
On Earth's curved path.
As we walk, you make me laugh,
While I restfully rest in truth,
It's to be with you.

Cause with you,
That's where I'm made stronger.

Holding on,
Holding on
To you.

Accepted Me

Colorfully crafted in beauty,
Beautifully black,
Created on time,
With purpose in mind.

Wonderfully sounded to the beat of Heaven's drums,
Overcoming attacks—
It's not fiction... it's facts
On black, beautiful ones.

Ancestors' scars,
Great courage,
I continue to stand.

Stand to be me,
Stand to be free in colorfully me,
Just as I am.

Important like all,
God created uniquely to be.

A race to face,
Love and acceptance for all,
Including me—
Black, beautiful,
Colorful me.

Attentive

Is there anyone that hears me,
While I sit in this pain?
Screaming loud while full of shame,
Unbelievable to me.

As I see the noses speaking,
They're better than me.
Body language spoken,
Giving hopelessness no rest.

Who will attend to the cries of me?
It's the Savior who supplies all I need.

.

Gift

God's great gift to me,
It is the gift I receive.
Such relief,
Oh banner of mine,
Abundantly,
Forever will
Be your will for me.

Great gift I receive.

Return

They squander the love I gave to them,
And yet it is my will
That they return to me,
The God they cannot see.

Knock, knock again,
Will you let me in?

Get cleansed from your sin of rebellion to me.
Oh, can't you see
My love only you need?
Let go of idolatry.

The world has had its fill,
And left you empty.

Return to me.
Come and receive my love, grace, mercy, and forgiveness
again—
All who have sinned and turned from me.

Says the Loving Savior

See my arms extended still.

Quenched

My cup is filled with your will.
How good it is to drink
From the foundation that quenches my thirst.

Forever True

Faithful to the few,
Faithful to all me,
To lovingly send
Jesus to save us from our sin.

Who will comprehend their need for Him?
He bled and died—
His story true.

He lay dead in the grave too,
Yet, on the 3rd day—
They can't take this away,
He rose up.

It wasn't tough,
Cause He's the God that does what He says He will do.

He led captivity captive
And gave gifts to men—
Restorer and the Forgiver of sin.

The Risen King—
Let the choir sing:
Salvation reign... forever true.

New Feet

Limbs lost,
Can't move.
But let your heart keep on walkin'.

No, this is not the end—
New learning over again.

There is a time to live,
And there is a time to die.
I've watched you cry.
Yes, and in this trial,
I have heard your earnest scream, *Why... me?*

Surprised with the answer,
Still—don't let go of me.
Let's do the hard new together.

For I'm taking you on an unexpected journey
With dis...abilities
 That don't disable my ability,
To help you through to the other side,
From tragedy to test..i..monies.

Oh, watch you move in me, if you let me.
Will you let me?

I understand you're mad at me—
I can handle the frustrated you,
That's mad at me too.

I've come to help.
Will you let me?

Carry the weight,
Cause what I have before you is great.

Let go and motion your heart,
Even when it seems everything is falling apart.

Let your faith take its new feet—
Walk on by faith.

Web

Hidden and small, the spider bit me.
When I woke up, it wasn't a dream.

I called for help, and no one heard me and my three,
Screaming, behind the brick walls.
The walls would not crumble
For me and my three.

Surely they would see—
See the wounded me and my three,
Wrapped on the spider's web.

No one could understand the translation
Because of the spirit of charm and manipulation
That was plaguing us all—
Me and my three and those in society
Who were supposed to help me,
But instead
Helped wrap the web of shame on me.

Me and my three,
Left lifeless on the spider's web,
Sucked by them all.

Can't Hide

Enemies prowling around your children,
To manipulate with hidden conversations as bait.
Masked compete and envy—
Lurking to gather information for pills for drama,
Drawing them from truth's blessing.

You see, that's what they will do
As they are dressed in pretend play of concern.

Lord, help my children discern
The true robbers and the thieves.

But yet, sure still, God sees every ill will
Of what they are doing to them
And doing to me.

Their downfall they shall eat of its cause.
When they come after them,
They come after me.

Oh, it is an appointed time,
Poisonous snakes cannot hide.

As it is appointed—
Don't you touch God's anointed,
'Cause it could cost your very life.

Poisonous snakes cannot hide.

Savior's Hall

As the Savior has appeared,
I will not fear.
I cast all—
This is my breakthrough year,
As I'm in my Savior's Hall.

Reach

Who do I give this pain?
Why does it seem like death is having its fame in my life?
It's hard to maintain.

When will it disappear?
I hear the Savior's near.

Soul of mine, get together—
Be of a good cheer
As I reach for Him right here.

It's Not About Me

Pride is the executioner to my spiritual consecration.
This is not meant to be.
Choked out my sanity—
True humility, remarry me.

As I drop down on my knees.

For my soul has learned,
It's all about you, God,
And not about me.

Face It

Fear had the nerve to slap me in my face
When I would no longer date its hate for me.

I mean... really?
You want to block me?
To stop me from walking on the water of the sea?

See, me and you aren't meant to be.
It's time for you to let go of me
And I let go of you,
To gain what's ordained for me—
My true destiny God has for me in prosperity.

So, if you want to be with me,
This can't be,
Cause this love thang
Only leads me to carnality,
Hindered causalities in my personality,
And not spiritual maturity.

You can go ahead, stand there and chill,
But I'm gonna take my will
And give it back to the man who gave it to me.

Fear, I realized I've lived with you too long—
Doubtful and paralyzed.

Accept it!
It's no more you and I.

I'm walkin'—faith-filled, surrendered,
With Jesus by my side.

Finally

He saw my worth for real.
He came after me.
He saw all of my rejection and gave affection.

That night I will never forget,
When my tears drained my pillowcases,
As I was intimate with restlessness...
On what should have been a heavenly resting place,
With my body at ease.

Instead, in those moments—
Before He came—
It was more of a place of disgrace,
Hidden from others, but not from Him.

He saw my heart,
That was torn apart from all the lies, deceit, and
tragedies.

In that hour came His rushing power
That caused me to drop down on my knees to His feet.
He stroked my head and rubbed my neck
While the stress pains vanished from me.

Finally found.
Why this couldn't be?
Such a man of honesty and character,
That spoke so eloquently and lovely to me—
Gently disarming every giant in the room that sent me
gloom.
They disappeared—
Right there, right there, in the room.

A listening ear that made my heart cheer,
Lovebirds chirping together in the room.
My belly leaping like a baby in the womb!

Life, growth, and change enveloped me.
Love announced its name!
Oh, true love came into the room!

Right there!
Right there in the room,
I saw flowers bloom!

He held me in His arms—
A chorus of a song sprang up out of me.

Finally,
This wonderful man—
He didn't pretend.
He truly cared about me.

Quality time for me;
Spoke right to the lonely me.
Shattered every kind of man's falsehood and hypocrisy.
Let me know—
Be of good cheer, dear. I am here.
And you have what I know you have been desiring:

Love, joy, peace, comfort,
And forever—My company.
Continue to feast from Me.

That one night in my room was so bright;
Causing my crying nights to become history,
And my pillows no longer soaked.

As that encounter was everything to me.
I was finally seen.
It wasn't a dream.

The Great Knight who stepped on the scene.
No other man can compare—
It was Jesus there.

Right there!
Right there!
Right there in the room.

Shout

Shouting in the church,
Electrified by the praise inside of me.
Oh, Sweet Jubilee has come!

Shouting in the church—
Can't stop shouting,
Can't sit still.

I... can't sit still.
I... can't sit still.

About the Author

Gwen Danwood was born and raised in a small town. She is a wife, mother of three, author, songwriter, and spoken word artist who is passionate about the arts. She discovered and embraced the beauty in the art of expressive writing to help improve her health, work through life's challenges and emotions, and build her resilience. She is graced with a mission to help others do the same. She mentors at-risk youth and help others in their time of crisis.

In her spare time, she enjoys spending time with family, decorating, watching old sitcoms, and viewing nature.

Dear Reader,

Before You Go…

If you've made it to this page, thank you for reading and for staying.

This book was never just about poetry. It was about breaking silence, facing pain, and making space for healing and wholeness. I pray the words spoke to your heart, reminding you that you're not alone, giving you strength to keep going, or inspiring you in some way. Whether you personally purchased this book, someone recommended it, or it was gifted to you, know that it was not an accident, but divine.

This collection was written in the quiet, raw moments when I had no words left, only tears. Some poems came when I didn't understand why I was writing, only that I was driven to. There were days I couldn't articulate the pain I was feeling to anyone. All I could do was pray, cry out to God, and write. The Holy Spirit led my hands, faithfully giving me the words when I had none, showing me that even in suffering, there is purpose.

Through all that I faced, Jesus has been my help, my refuge, my steady place, my joy, my strength, my comfort, my friend, my rescuer, my lifeline, and my love line.

If you've known sorrow, or if you're still in it, I pray these words meet you with grace and inspire you in some way. You are not alone. You are loved and prayed for. Don't give up. Despite the pain and challenges, everything has its season.

Let this be your reminder:
Pain does not get the final word.
Healing and wholeness are yours to receive.
Hope still belongs to you.

Walk forward knowing your transformation will come. There are new and greater chapters ahead in your life. Someone needs your voice, your story, your choice, and your uniqueness. You are a valuable asset on Earth.

With love,
Gwen

"He heals the brokenhearted and binds up their wounds." —
Psalm 147:3

www.ingramcontent.com/pod-product-compliance
Lightning Source LLC
Chambersburg PA
CBHW051234120626
46547CB00013B/1642